Forest
Friends

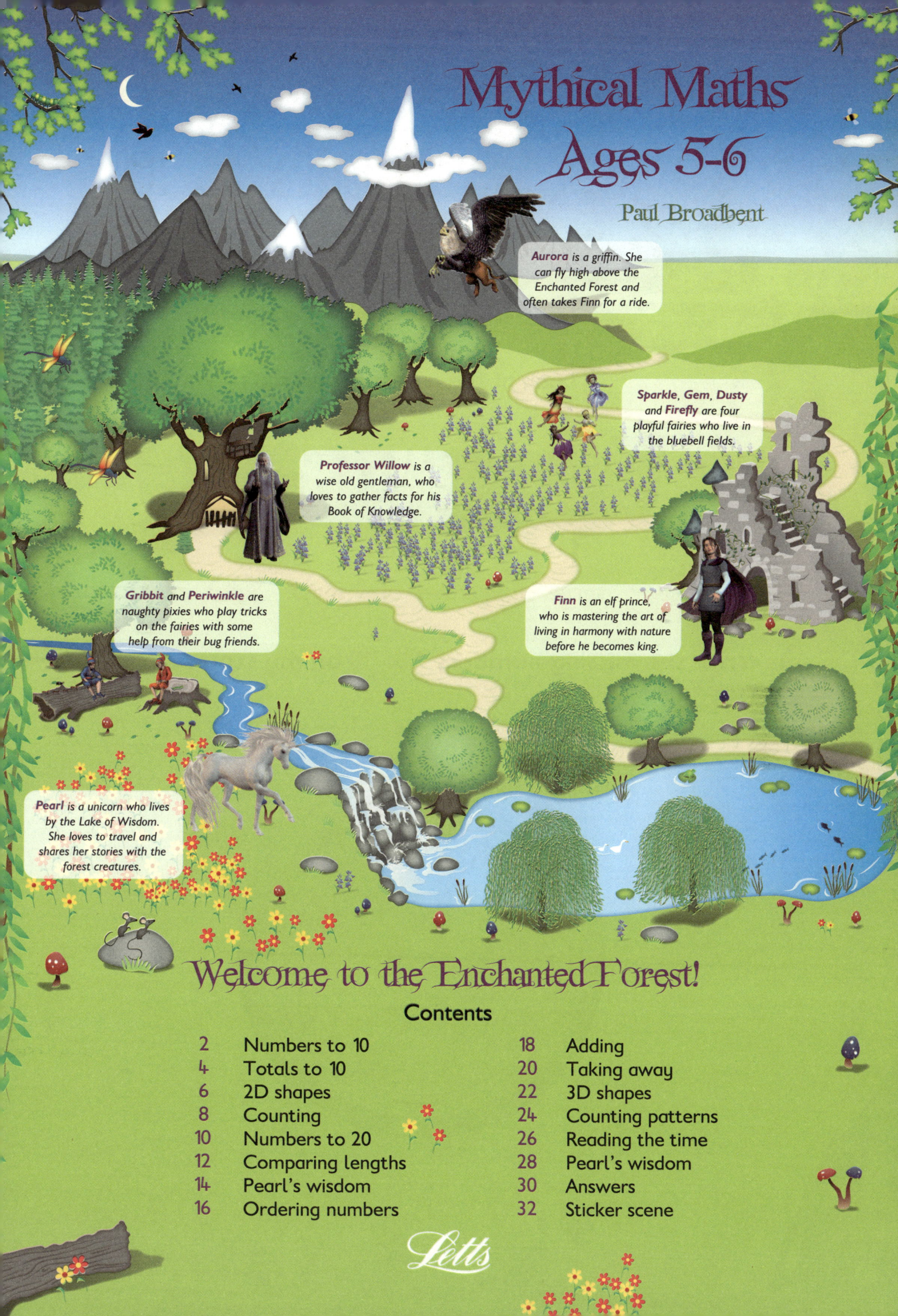

Mythical Maths
Ages 5-6

Paul Broadbent

Aurora is a griffin. She can fly high above the Enchanted Forest and often takes Finn for a ride.

Sparkle, Gem, Dusty and *Firefly* are four playful fairies who live in the bluebell fields.

Professor Willow is a wise old gentleman, who loves to gather facts for his Book of Knowledge.

Gribbit and *Periwinkle* are naughty pixies who play tricks on the fairies with some help from their bug friends.

Finn is an elf prince, who is mastering the art of living in harmony with nature before he becomes king.

Pearl is a unicorn who lives by the Lake of Wisdom. She loves to travel and shares her stories with the forest creatures.

Welcome to the Enchanted Forest!

Contents

Letts

Numbers to 10

I am Professor Willow. Let's start by looking at the numbers **1** to **10** in my Book of Knowledge.

Look at the numbers and say them aloud.

| 1 | 2 | 3 | 4 | 5 | 6 | 7 | 8 | 9 | 10 |

one   two   three   four   five   six   seven   eight   nine   ten

1 **Write the missing numbers 1 to 10 on my stopwatch. Tick-tock!**

 Join each number to the matching word. If at first you do not succeed, try, try again!

| 5 | 1 | 7 | 2 | 3 | 8 | 4 | 6 | 10 | 9 |

two   five   one   three   seven   nine   six   ten   four   eight

 Wonderful work! Now write in the missing numbers.

a   1   2   3   ☐   5   ☐   7   8   9   10

b   ☐   2   3   4   5   6   7   8   9   ☐

c   1   ☐   ☐   4   5   6   7   8   9   10

d   1   2   3   4   ☐   6   ☐   8   9   10

Willow's Quest

Follow the numbers and join these dots in order, to reveal a new number. It is as easy as 1-2-3!

2   3   3   2   1
1   4   4
6   5   6
6 5 4   5   7
7   10   8
11 ·9   9
10

Place the sticker of my Book of Knowledge on the map on the last page of this book.

Totals to 10

I am Finn. Let's focus on these leaves by adding the piles together.

You add things by putting them together.

This will give you a total.

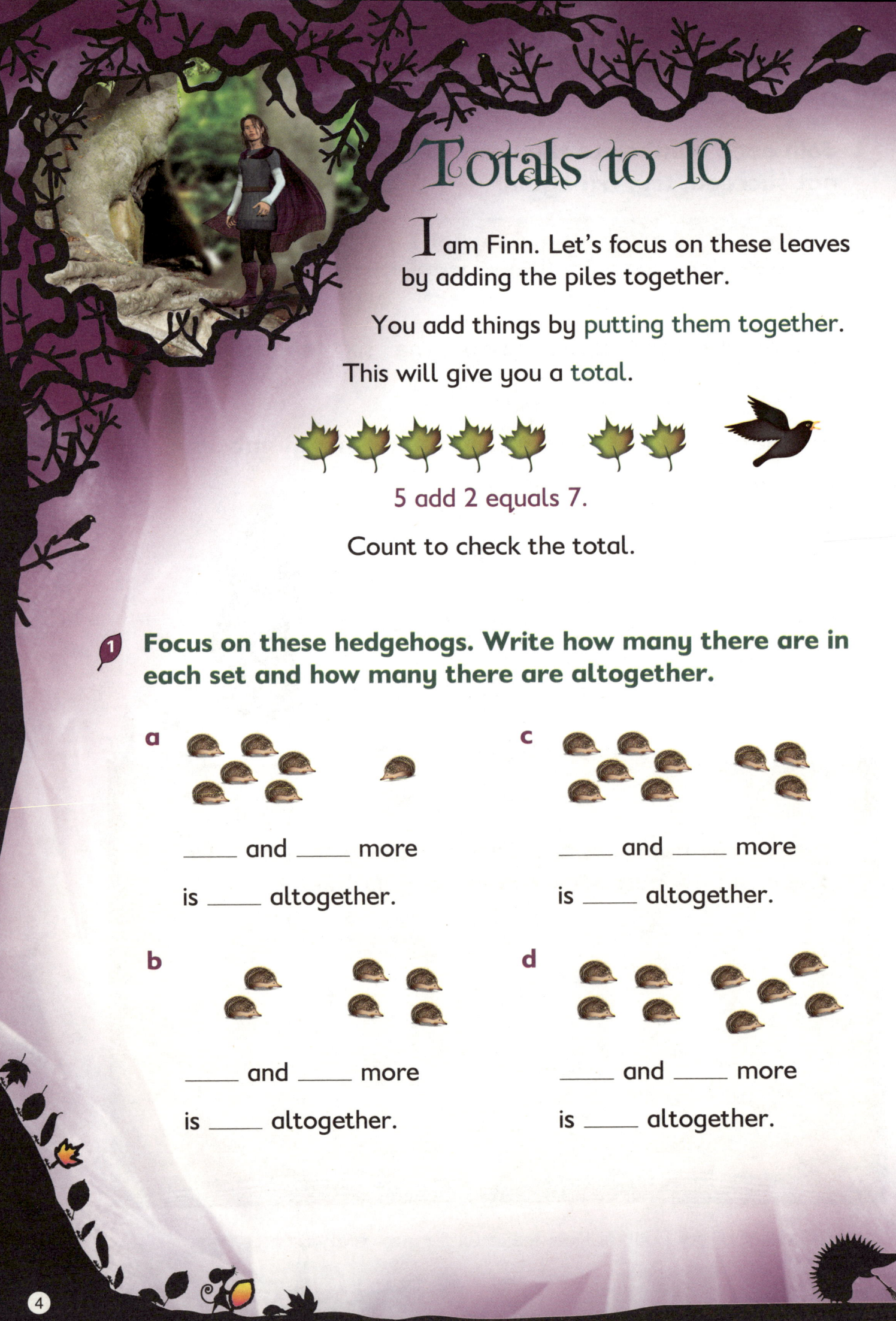

5 add 2 equals 7.

Count to check the total.

1 **Focus on these hedgehogs. Write how many there are in each set and how many there are altogether.**

a

_____ and _____ more

is _____ altogether.

b

_____ and _____ more

is _____ altogether.

c

_____ and _____ more

is _____ altogether.

d

_____ and _____ more

is _____ altogether.

2 Write the total for each of these, maths warrior.

a   ✳ ✳ ✳   +   ✳ ✳ ✳   = ☐

b   ✳   +   ✳ ✳ ✳ ✳ ✳ ✳   = ☐

c   ✳ ✳ ✳ ✳ ✳   +   ✳ ✳ ✳   = ☐

d   ✳ ✳   +   ✳ ✳   = ☐

e   ✳ ✳ ✳   +   ✳ ✳   = ☐

f   ✳ ✳ ✳ ✳   +   ✳ ✳ ✳ ✳   = ☐

3 Balance is the key to success. Add 3 to each of these numbers.

a   4 add 3 equals ____   d   3 add 3 equals ____

b   2 add 3 equals ____   e   1 add 3 equals ____

c   5 add 3 equals ____   f   6 add 3 equals ____

Willow's Quest

Colour the leaves with a total of 9 in yellow.
Colour the leaves with a total of 6 in red.

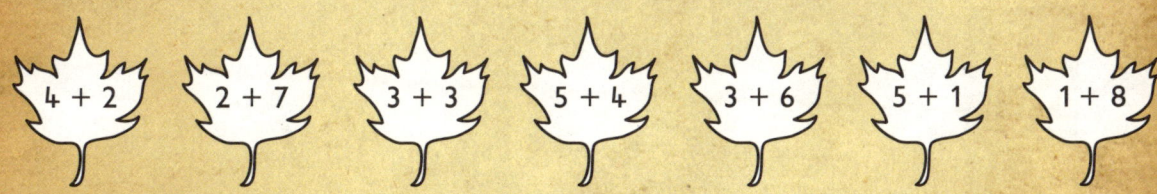

4 + 2   2 + 7   3 + 3   5 + 4   3 + 6   5 + 1   1 + 8

Write how many leaves of each colour there are and how many there are altogether.

_____ yellow leaves and _____ red leaves is _____ altogether.

Put the hedgehogs sticker on the map!

2D shapes

We are Periwinkle and Gribbit. We will soon get your maths into shape!

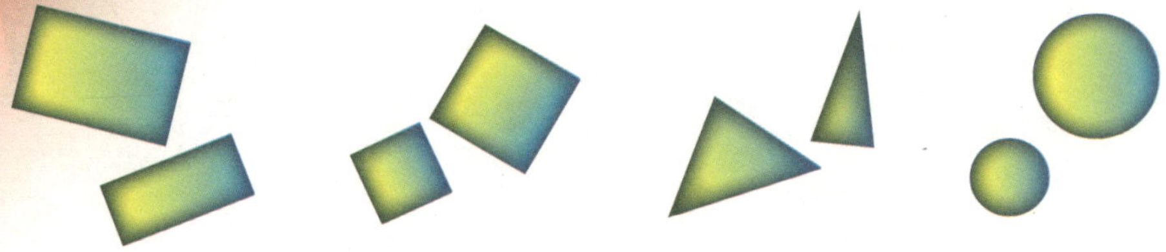

Rectangles   Squares   Triangles   Circles

Have a go at comparing these squelchy shapes.
How are they the same? How are they different?

1 Let's get busy! Draw a line to join each shape to its name.

rectangle

circle

square

triangle

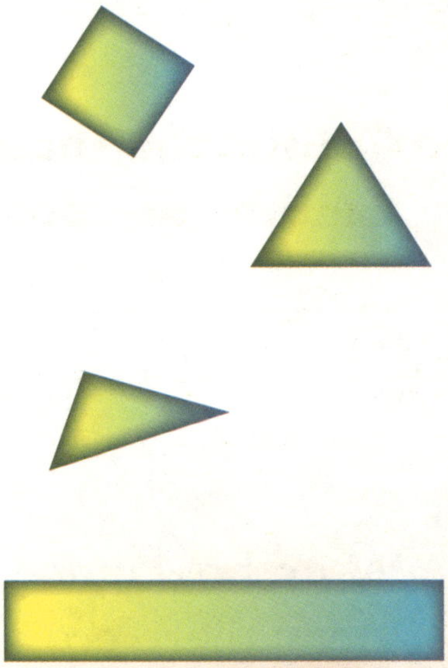

2 Can you find the odd shape out in each set, smarty-pants? Cross through the shape that is different.

a

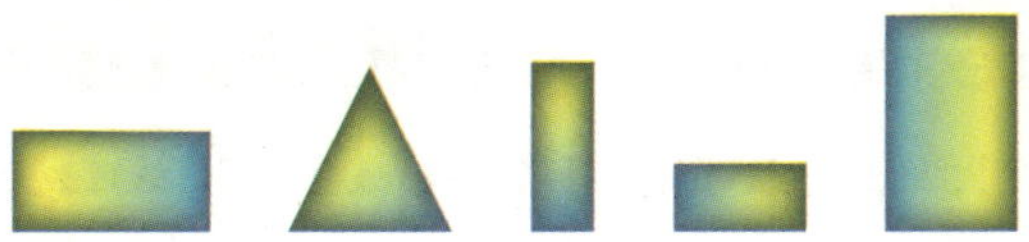

c

b

d

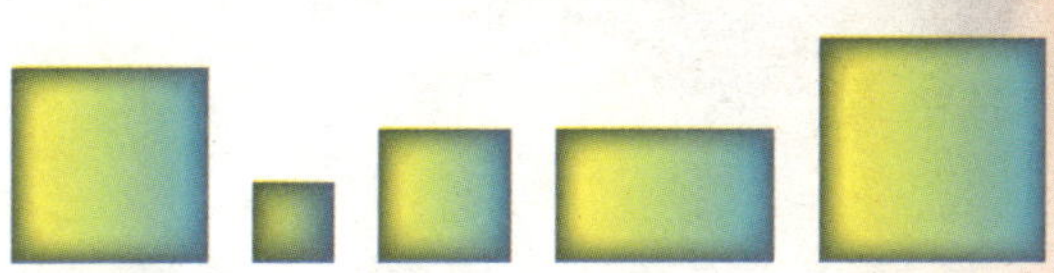

3 Bring on the bugs! Write the name of each shape made by these spiders.

a   b   c   d

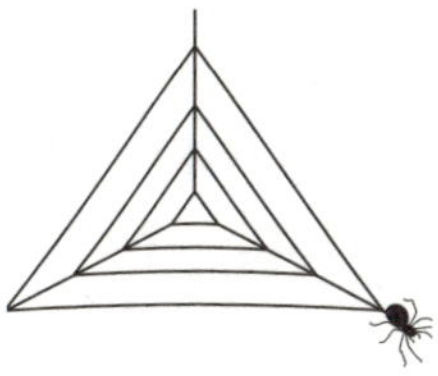

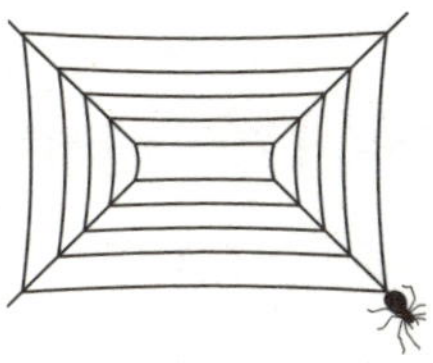

_____ _____ _____ _____

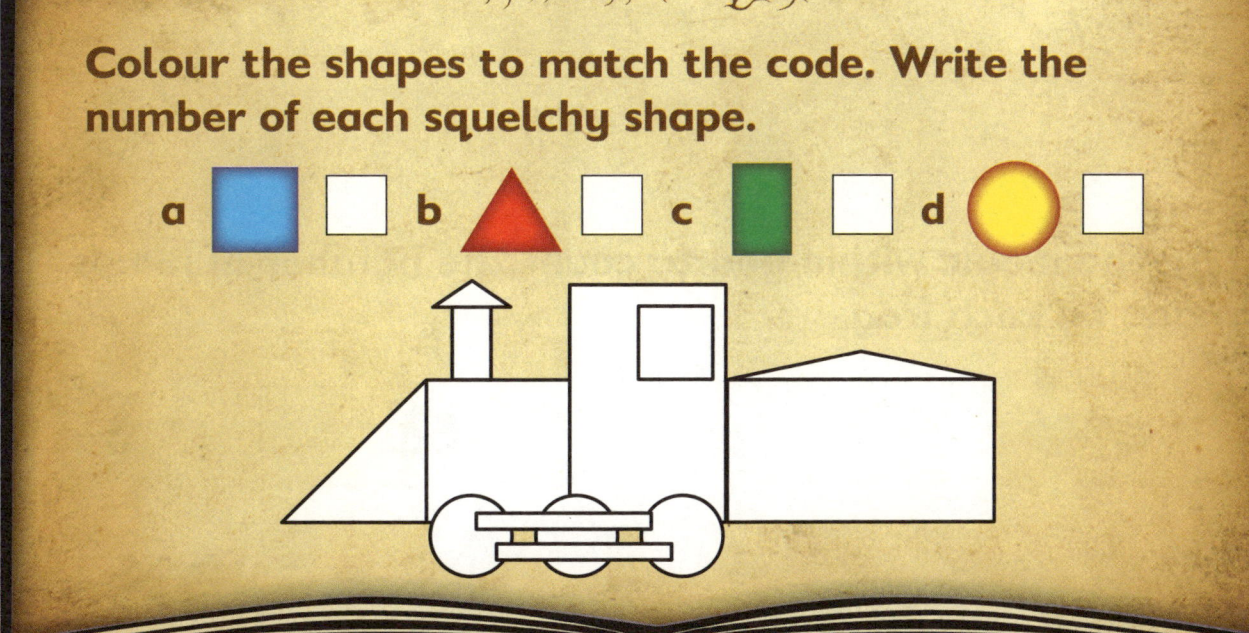

Willow's Quest

Colour the shapes to match the code. Write the number of each squelchy shape.

a [blue square] [ ]   b [red triangle] [ ]   c [green rectangle] [ ]   d [yellow circle] [ ]

Bugalicious! Put the picnic sticker on the map.

7

Counting

I am Pearl and I live by the Lake of Wisdom. Let's begin by learning to count. Look carefully and count the number of spots on each ladybird. Say the numbers aloud.

| 11 | 12 | 13 | 14 | 15 | 16 | 17 | 18 | 19 | 20 |

1 Draw the correct number of spots on each ladybird. Then colour them in your favourite colour!

a

11

b

17

c

14

2 Use the magic within you to count the number of jumps made by each frog.

a

b

8

3 Count how many of each object there are in the Lake of Wisdom.

a  ☐

b  ☐

c  ☐

d  ☐

Willow's Quest

Now count the number of spoons on each of my water wheels.

a   b   c   d

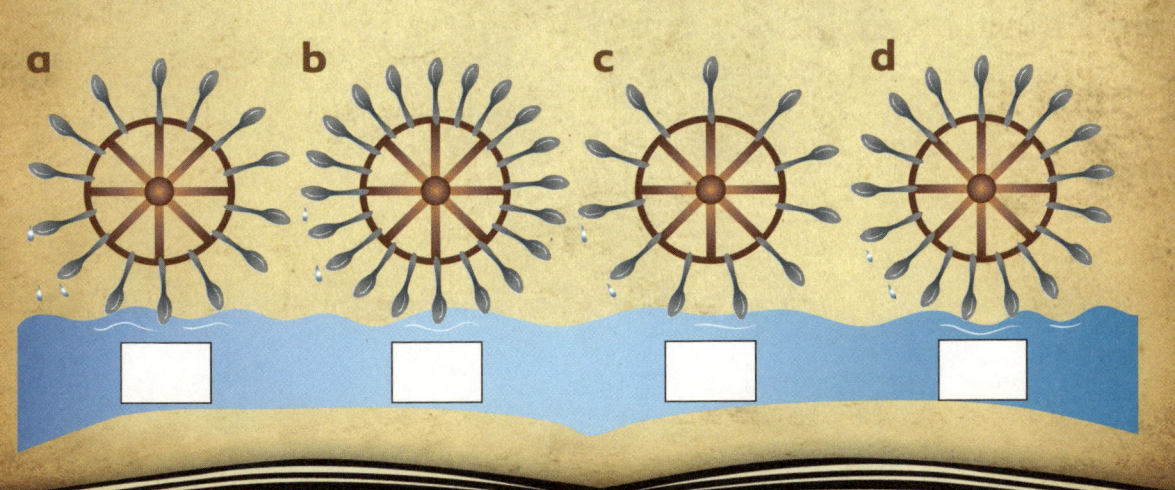

Place the frog sticker on the map.

Numbers to 20

I am going to help you to focus on teen numbers.

The numbers from 13 to 19 are teen numbers. They are all made from a ten and ones and end in… teen! 11 and 12 are made from a ten and ones but do not end in teen.

11 10 and 1
eleven

14 10 and 4
fourteen

17 10 and 7
seventeen

12 10 and 2
twelve

15 10 and 5
fifteen

18 10 and 8
eighteen

13 10 and 3
thirteen

16 10 and 6
sixteen

19 10 and 9
nineteen

1 **Now try these, number warrior. Write the number to match each word.**

a fourteen

d fifteen

b twelve

e eighteen

c seventeen

f thirteen

2 Balance is the key to success for this task. Write the missing numbers to make each statement true.

a 10 + 3 = ☐

c ☐ + 9 = 19

b 10 + ☐ = 11

d 10 + 6 = ☐

3 Search for the truth behind these pictures. Draw lines to join each dot-to-dot.

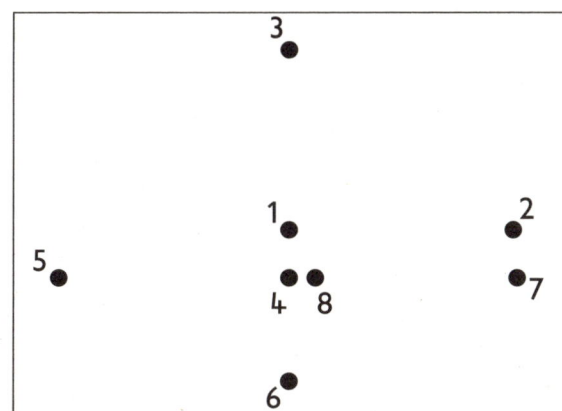
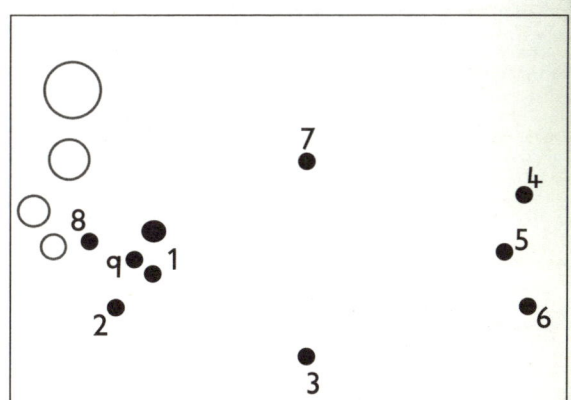

Willow's Quest

Write these numbers as words to complete this puzzle.

15

12

11

17

18

y

What is the secret number? _____

Now you have mastered numbers, place the sticker of the  treasure chest on the map.

Comparing lengths

We are Gem and Sparkle. We will help you to compare the lengths of different objects.

Look at these unicorn horns. Magic!

Shortest   Short   Long   Longest

1 Dazzle us with your drawing and complete Pearl. Follow the instructions.

a Draw a short horn on Pearl.   **b** Draw a long tail on Pearl.

2 Let's tidy up these sledges! Circle the **longest** sledge in each set.

a

c

b

d

3 Wave your wand and circle the **shortest** snowman in each set.

a

c

b

d

Willow's Quest

Draw a line from each word to the correct flag.

a   b   c   d

shortest   short   long   longest

Pop the unicorns on the map.

Pearl's wisdom

1 Take your time and write the missing numbers in each set.

a 1 2 3 ☐ ☐ 6 7 ☐ 9 10

b ☐ ☐ 3 4 5 6 7 8 9 ☐

c 1 2 ☐ 4 5 ☐ ☐ 8 ☐ 10

2 Swish, swish! write the total for each.

a

3 + 2 = ☐

b

1 + 6 = ☐

c

5 + 4 = ☐

d

2 + 2 = ☐

e

4 + 3 = ☐

f

6 + 2 = ☐

3 Use the magic within you to join each shape to its name.

square   circle   rectangle   triangle

4 **Count these shells carefully.**

a

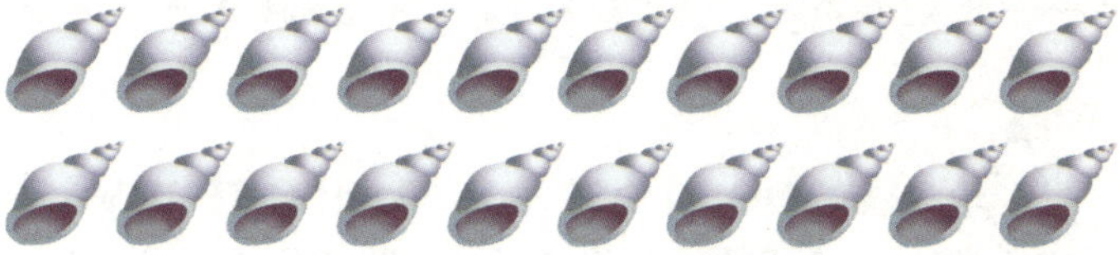

b

c

d

5 **Write the teen numbers for each of these. The Lake of Wisdom holds the answers!**

a 10 + 4 =

b 10 + 8 =

c 10 + 3 =

d 10 + 9 =

e 10 + 6 =

f 10 + 5 =

6 **Look at the lengths in each set and join them to the correct word.**

a

shortest   short   long   longest

b

shortest   short   long   longest

Swish, swish! Place the shells sticker on the map.

Ordering numbers

A number track is a great invention. It will help you to learn the order of numbers.

Cover some numbers with your fingers. Which ones are hidden?

1 Some of the numbers have fallen off these number tracks. Write each number in the correct order. No time like the present!

a

7			10	11		

12	9	13	8

b

12	13			16		

14	17	15	18

c

		12	13	14		

16	15	11	10

d

2	3			6		

4	8	7	5

e

13		15		17		

16	19	14	18

Write the next two numbers in each sequence.

a | 11 | 12 | 13 | 14 | | |

d | 15 | 16 | 17 | 18 | | |

b | 6 | 7 | 8 | 9 | | |

e | 8 | 9 | 10 | 11 | | |

c | 2 | 3 | 4 | 5 | | |

f | 14 | 15 | 16 | 17 | | |

 Here are some numbers from my Book of Knowledge. Write them in the correct order.

a | 10 | 8 | 11 | 7 | 9 |

c | 6 | 3 | 5 | 4 | 7 |

b | 16 | 20 | 19 | 17 | 18 |

d | 11 | 15 | 13 | 14 | 12 |

Willow's Quest

Tick-tock! These boxes should be in number order, but two have swapped places. Circle the two boxes that are not in order.

a | 4 | 2 | 3 | 1 | 5 |

c | 16 | 20 | 18 | 19 | 17 |

b | 11 | 12 | 15 | 14 | 13 |

d | 8 | 9 | 11 | 10 | 12 |

Wonderful work! Place the squirrel and rabbit sticker on the map.

Adding

Use the number line to help you add.
It helps us to add faster than the fairies!
Start at 4 and count on 5.

0 1 2 3 4 5 6 7 8 9 10

$4 + 5 = 9$

We use the $+$ sign to show adding. $=$ is the equals sign.

4   +   5   =   9

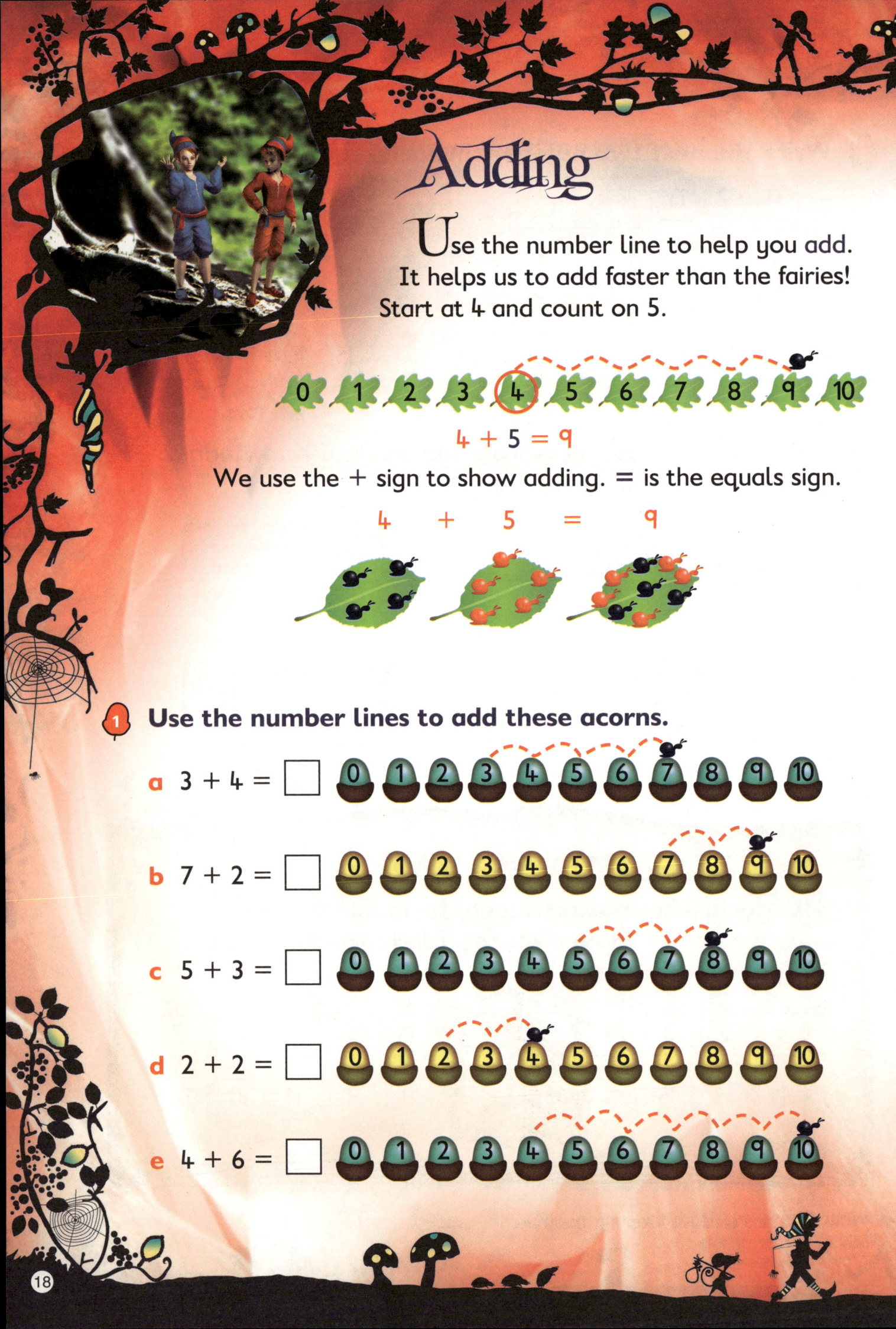

1 **Use the number lines to add these acorns.**

a $3 + 4 = \Box$ 0 1 2 3 4 5 6 7 8 9 10

b $7 + 2 = \Box$ 0 1 2 3 4 5 6 7 8 9 10

c $5 + 3 = \Box$ 0 1 2 3 4 5 6 7 8 9 10

d $2 + 2 = \Box$ 0 1 2 3 4 5 6 7 8 9 10

e $4 + 6 = \Box$ 0 1 2 3 4 5 6 7 8 9 10

2 **Draw the jumps on each number line. Then write in the answer.**

a 4 + 2 = ☐ 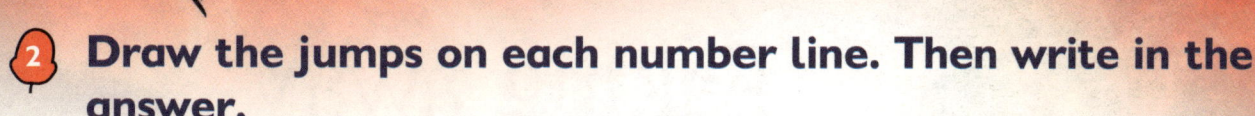 0 1 2 3 4 5 6 7 8 9 10

b 6 + 3 = ☐ 0 1 2 3 4 5 6 7 8 9 10

c 7 + 1 = ☐ 0 1 2 3 4 5 6 7 8 9 10

d 5 + 5 = ☐ 0 1 2 3 4 5 6 7 8 9 10

3 **Now try these additions. Bugalicious!**

a 2 + 3 = ☐   e 8 + 1 = ☐

b 4 + 4 = ☐   f 6 + 2 = ☐

c 5 + 2 = ☐   g 9 + 0 = ☐

d 7 + 3 = ☐   h 8 + 2 = ☐

Willow's Quest

Use the number machine to add these sums.

a 4

b 3

IN  OUT →

c 6

d 5

e 7

☐
☐
☐
☐
☐

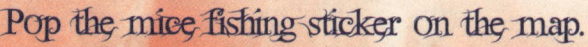 Pop the mice fishing sticker on the map.

Taking away

It is time to learn about taking away. Look carefully and you will see that we use the – sign when we subtract or take away.

$$6 - 2 = 4$$

start with 6   take away 2   left 4

🌸 **Take away and then write how many ladybirds are left in these sums.**

a

5 – 3 = ☐

b

4 – 2 = ☐

c

6 – 1 = ☐

d

5 – 4 = ☐

e

7 – 3 = ☐

f

3 – 0 = ☐

2 Cross out some toadstools to help you take away.

a 3 – 1 = ☐   b 5 – 2 = ☐   c 7 – 4 = ☐

3 Swish, swish! Take away 2 and find the answer. Join each leaf to the ladybird with the correct answer.

3 – 2   1   8 – 2   4   2 – 2

3   6 – 2   2   5 – 2   6

9 – 2   0   5   7   7 – 2

4 – 2

Willow's Quest

Write out a subtraction for each of these toadstool sums.

a   ☐ – ☐ = ☐

b   ☐ – ☐ = ☐

c   ☐ – ☐ = ☐

d   ☐ – ☐ = ☐

 Put the bluebells sticker on the map.

3D shapes

We are Dusty and Firefly. Look at the shapes of objects around you. Magic!

What makes them the same?
What makes them different?

Swirl some fairy dust over these shapes and try to remember their names.

Cuboid　　　**Cube**　　　**Sphere**　　　**Cone**　　　**Cylinder**

⭐ **Wave your wand and join each shape to its name.**

cylinder

cube

sphere

cone

cuboid

2 Let's tidy up and match each shadow to its shape.

3 Circle the odd shape out in each set.

a

b

c

d

e

f

Willow's Quest

Flit, flit! Write the shape name of these everyday objects.

a

b

c

d

_____   _____

Counting patterns

I am Aurora. Fly with me to count forwards and backwards.

The sky is the limit with counting patterns!

| 7 | 8 | 9 | 10 | 11 | 12 |

| 19 | 18 | 17 | 16 | 15 | 14 |

Counting patterns can help you to work out missing numbers.

13   14   15   ?   17   ?

The missing numbers are 16 and 18.

1 **Count forwards or backwards to continue these patterns. Write the next two numbers in each pattern.**

a   11   12   13   14   15

b   6   7   8   9   10

c   14   15   16   17   18

d   8   7   6   5   4

2 **You are flying through this! Write in the missing numbers in each counting pattern.**

a   [ ]   8   9   [ ]   11   12

b   [ ]   14   [ ]   16   17   18

c   12   [ ]   10   9   [ ]   7

d   [ ]   [ ]   18   17   16   15

e   [ ]   13   12   11   10   [ ]

3 **You are a star! Write the missing numbers on this grid.**

	2	3	4	
6		8	9	10
11	12			15
16		18		20

Willow's Quest

Write the missing numbers on Professor Willow's stopwatch and then write the missing page numbers.

a

b

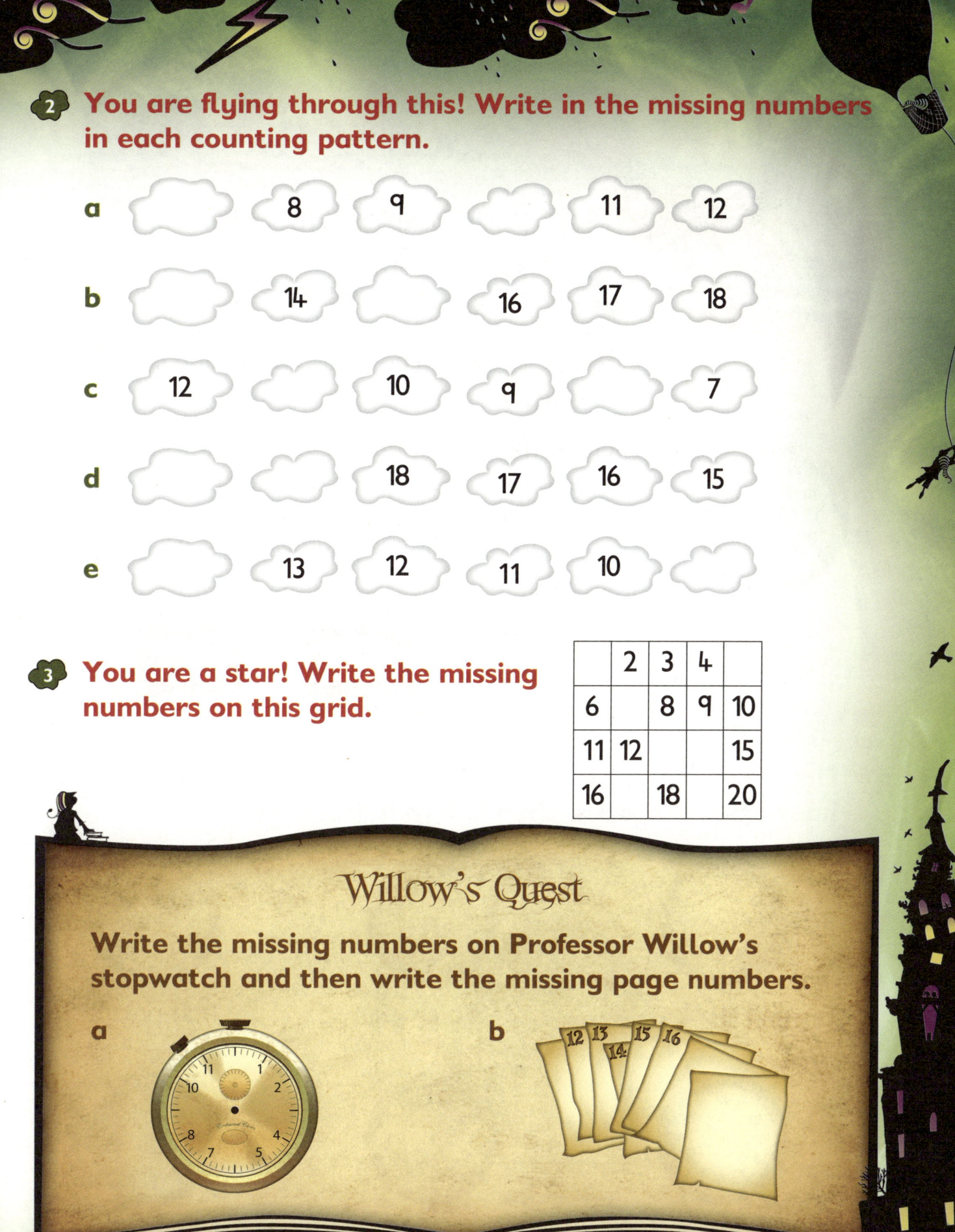

Place the flock of birds sticker on the map.

Reading the time

Tick-tock! This clock shows 8 o'clock.
- The long minute hand is pointing to 12, so it is an o'clock time.
- The short hour hand is pointing to 8, so it is 8 o'clock.

This clock shows half past 8.
- The long minute hand is pointing to 6, so it is a half past time.
- The short hour hand is pointing past 8, so it is half past 8.

These are the same times on a digital clock: 8 o'clock.

08:00   20:00

1 **Draw the correct time on each clock. Make sure that the hour hand is shorter than the minute hand.**

a
7 o'clock

b
9 o'clock

c
half past 1

d
half past 10

e
3 o'clock

f
half past 2

2 **Now write out these times using o'clock or half past.**

a

_____

b

_____

c

_____

d

_____

e

_____

f

_____

Willow's Quest

Complete the Book of Knowledge by writing in the missing times.

 **a**  **b**  **c**  **d**  **e**

Today I started work on my Book of Knowledge at **a** ____ o'clock. At half past **b** ____ I went out for a walk. I began to mend the Maths Machine at **c** ____ o'clock. Finn cooked a wonderful dinner at half past **d** ____ and I went to bed at half past **e** ____. I was very tired after my busy day.

Put the dragonflies sticker on the map. No time like the present!

Pearl's wisdom

1 Take your time and write the next two numbers in these sequences.

a 5 6 7 8 ☐ ☐   d 7 8 9 10 ☐ ☐

b 1 2 3 4 ☐ ☐   e 15 16 17 18 ☐ ☐

c 13 14 15 16 ☐ ☐   f 9 10 11 12 ☐ ☐

2 Use the number line to help you add up the sums. You can do this with a swish of your tail!

a 4 + 3 = ☐   b 6 + 2 = ☐   c 3 + 1 = ☐

d 5 + 5 = ☐   e 7 + 2 = ☐   f 4 + 5 = ☐

3 Use the magic within you to take away. Cross out the fish to help you.

a 8 – 2 = ☐

b 4 – 1 = ☐

c 6 – 3 = ☐

d 9 – 4 = ☐

e 7 – 5 = ☐

4 Find the odd shape out in each set and write its name.

a  c

_____   _____

b  d

_____   _____

5 Swish, swish! Count forwards or backwards and write the missing numbers in these counting patterns.

a

3		5	6		8	

c

16	15	14		12	

b

12	13		15		17

d

		18	17	16	15

6 Use o'clock or half past to write the times shown on each clock.

a  b  c

_____   _____   _____

d  e  f

_____   _____   _____

Place the crystals sticker on the map. Now your picture is complete!

Answers

Pages 2–3

1

2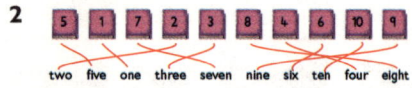

3 a 4, 6
  b 1, 10
  c 2, 3
  d 5, 7

Willow's Quest

The number is 35. Check that the dots are joined in order.

Pages 4–5

1 a 6 and 1 more is 7 altogether.
  b 2 and 4 more is 6 altogether.
  c 6 and 3 more is 9 altogether.
  d 4 and 5 more is 9 altogether.

2 a 6
  b 7
  c 8
  d 4
  e 5
  f 8

3 a 7
  b 5
  c 8
  d 6
  e 4
  f 9

Willow's Quest

4 yellow leaves and 3 red leaves is 7 altogether.

Pages 6–7

1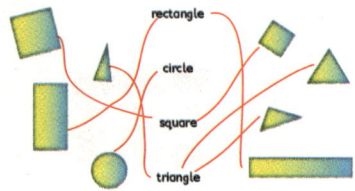

2 These are the odd shapes out:

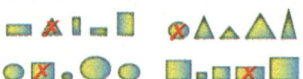

(continued)

3 a square
  b triangle
  c circle
  d rectangle

Willow's Quest

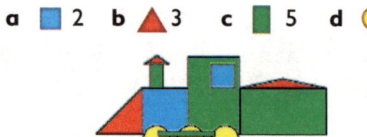

Pages 8–9

1 Check that the correct number of spots has been drawn on each ladybird.

2 a 12
  b 16

3 a 16 frogs
  b 13 flowers
  c 20 lily pad leaves
  d 18 fish

Willow's Quest

a 14
b 20
c 11
d 17

Pages 10–11

1 a 14
  b 12
  c 17
  d 15
  e 18
  f 13

2 a 13
  b 1
  c 10
  d 16

3 Check that the numbers have been followed in order.

Willow's Quest

15	f	i	f	t	e	e	n	
12			t	w	e	l	v	e
11			e	l	e	v	e	n
17	s	e	v	e	n	t	e	e	n
18	e	i	g	h	t	e	e	n
				y				

The secret number is 20

Pages 12–13

1 a Check that a short horn has been drawn.

  b Check that a long tail has been drawn.

2 a
  b
  c
  d

3 a
  b
  c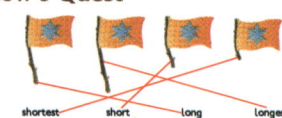
  d

Willow's Quest

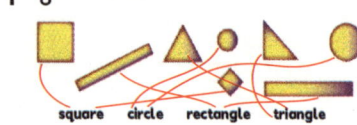

Pages 14–15

1 a 4, 5, 8
  b 1, 2, 10
  c 3, 6, 7, 9

2 a 5
  b 7
  c 9
  d 4
  e 7
  f 8

3

4 a 20
  b 15
  c 12
  d 17

5 a 14
  b 18
  c 13
  d 19
  e 16
  f 15

6

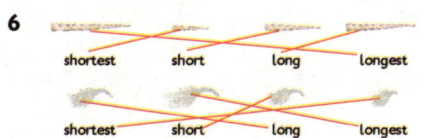

shortest   short   long   longest

shortest   short   long   longest

Pages 16–17

1 a | 7 | 8 | 9 | 10 | 11 | 12 | 13 |

b | 12 | 13 | 14 | 15 | 16 | 17 | 18 |

c | 10 | 11 | 12 | 13 | 14 | 15 | 16 |

d | 2 | 3 | 4 | 5 | 6 | 7 | 8 |

e | 13 | 14 | 15 | 16 | 17 | 18 | 19 |

2 a 15, 16
  b 10, 11
  c 6, 7
  d 19, 20
  e 12, 13
  f 18, 19

3 a 7, 8, 9, 10, 11
  b 16, 17, 18, 19, 20
  c 3, 4, 5, 6, 7
  d 11, 12, 13, 14, 15

Willow's Quest

a 4 and 1
b 15 and 13
c 20 and 17
d 11 and 10

Pages 18–19

1 a 7
  b 9
  c 8
  d 4
  e 10
2 a 6
  b 9
  c 8
  d 10
3 a 5
  b 8
  c 7
  d 10
  e 9
  f 8
  g 9
  h 10

Willow's Quest

a 7
b 6
c 9
d 8
e 10

Pages 20–21

1 a 2
  b 2
  c 5

d 1
e 4
f 3
2 a 2
  b 3
  c 3
3 3 – 2 = 1
  8 – 2 = 6
  2 – 2 = 0
  9 – 2 = 7
  6 – 2 = 4
  5 – 2 = 3
  4 – 2 = 2
  7 – 2 = 5

Willow's Quest

a 7 – 1 = 6
b 4 – 2 = 2
c 6 – 4 = 2
d 3 – 2 = 1

Pages 22–23

1

cylinder   cube   sphere

cone   cuboid

2

3 The odd shape in each set is:
  a sphere
  b cube
  c cylinder
  d cube
  e cylinder
  f cuboid

Willow's Quest

a cone
b cube
c sphere
d cuboid

Pages 24–25

1 a 16, 17
  b 11, 12
  c 19, 20
  d 3, 2
2 a 7, 10
  b 13, 15
  c 11, 8
  d 20, 19
  e 14, 9
3

1	2	3	4	5
6	7	8	9	10
11	12	13	14	15
16	17	18	19	20

Willow's Quest

a 3, 6, 9, 12
b 11, 17, 18

Pages 26–27

1

2 a 2 o'clock
  b 10 o'clock
  c half past 4
  d half past 11
  e 5 o'clock
  f half past 3

Willow's Quest

a 9 o'clock
b half past 10
c 2 o'clock
d half past 6
e half past 9

Pages 28–29

1 a 9, 10
  b 5, 6
  c 17, 18
  d 11, 12
  e 19, 20
  f 13, 14
2 a 7
  b 8
  c 4
  d 10
  e 9
  f 9
3 a 6
  b 3
  c 3
  d 5
  e 2
4 The odd shape in each set is:
  a cone
  b cube
  c cylinder
  d cuboid
5 a 4, 7
  b 14, 16
  c 13, 11
  d 20, 19
6 a 4 o'clock
  b half past 9
  c half past 2
  d 6 o'clock
  e half past 12
  f half past 9

Welcome to the Enchanted Forest...

Wonderful work!

Enchanted Forest Map Stickers

Extra Stickers